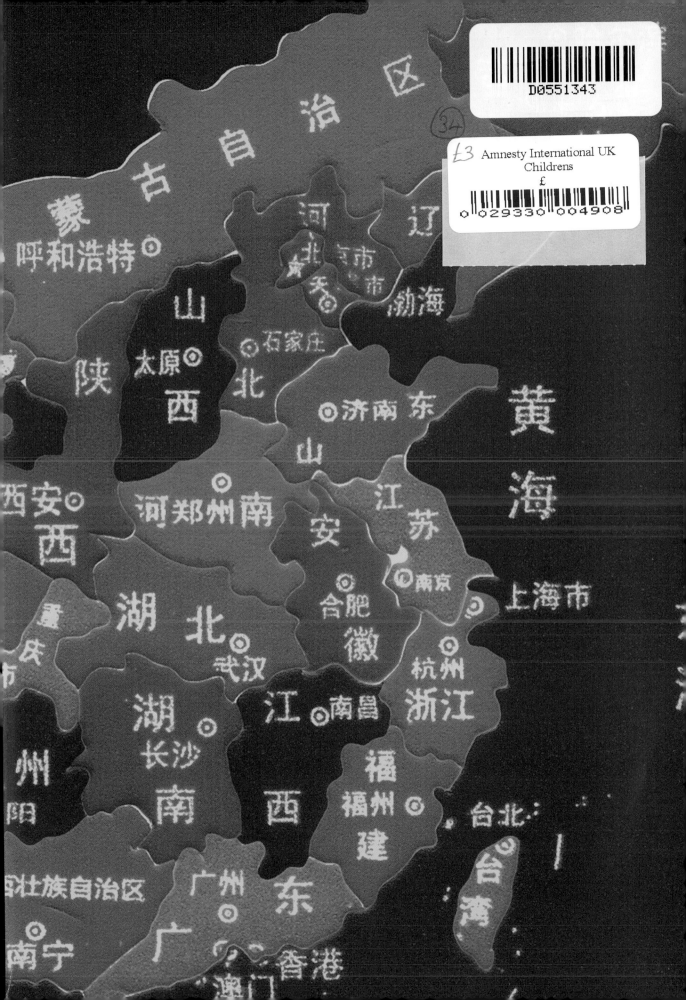

To "Rose" Zhang Qiang, "Stone" Shi Hailin, Sem Dui, and Sem Chang, and to Dimitri

Series Editors:

Laure Mistral
Philippe Godard

Also Available:

We Live in India

By Pascal Pilon and Élisabeth Thomas

We Live in

China

Illustrations by Sophie Duffet

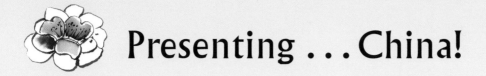 # Presenting ... China!

Surface Area: 3,696,502 square miles, about the same size as the United States (3,717,142 square miles). China is the one of the four largest countries in the world, behind the U.S., Canada, and Russia.

Population: China has the largest population in the world, with 1,306,313,000 inhabitants counted in the 2002 census. This is more than one fifth of the total population of the planet. China is home to 56 ethnic groups (or "peoples"). The Han ethnic group forms the majority (92 percent) of the total Chinese population. The other 55 groups are called "ethnic minorities." Of these, 18 include more than 1 million people each, and some even have their own languages and systems of writing.

Population Density: As calculated for the entire nation, population density comes to 344 people per square mile. But specific geographic differences are quite extreme: In the east, you find heavily populated cities (also called "megalopolises"), but the western part of the country has a very low density. At the low end of the spectrum, a number of regions are composed of barren desert.

China's Main Cities:
Beijing (called "Peking" in the past), the capital: about 14 million people.
Shanghai: about 16 million people.
Tianjin: 8.8 million people.

Climate: When you consider the total land mass and the diversity of the Chinese topography, you'll notice that there isn't just one climate. The weather ranges from the hot, humid climate of the tropical Sichuan region to the cold, arid weather that hangs endlessly over the mountains of Tibet.

Agricultural Products: Rice, wheat, potatoes, sorghum, corn, rapeseed, peanuts, tea, millet, barley, and cotton.

Unemployment: The unemployment rate is 10 percent in the urban settings, and 30 percent in the rural areas.

Money: The yuan, or renminbi ("people's currency").

Some History . . .

For **centuries,** China remained a mysterious place to outsiders. Westerners first became acquainted with it through the voyages of Marco Polo, an Italian merchant who lived during the thirteenth century. He remained in China for about twenty years as a servant of the emperor. Upon his return, he recounted fabulous adventures, not all of which were entirely true. But his tales of palaces built of gold and boundless treasures evoked daydreams in the minds of the Europeans. As a result, the trade of goods between Europe and China began to grow. Because the emperors wished to keep their country closed to outsiders and there was a tremendous distance people had to travel between lands, trade between Europe and China developed slowly.

During the nineteenth century, the British, French, Americans, Japanese, and Germans came to recognize that progress in China lagged significantly behind their own advances, especially in the field of military might and skill. In fact, their armies were much more powerful than the Chinese forces. Action soon followed: These Western nations partitioned the country into spheres of foreign influence, and then looted it.

In 1911, those Chinese who were open to the modernization of their nation struck back. They abolished the empire and set up a republic. What followed was an era of tumult and turmoil, during which Japan held sway over the country. After the Second World War and the defeat of Japan, the Chinese Communists, headed by Mao Zedong, assumed power. They established the People's Republic of China in 1949, a revolutionary act of major proportions for the country. The goal of eliminating poverty led leaders to do away with all private property and to divide up the land among the farmers. At the same time, the state took over control of private businesses. As a result, all Chinese now worked for the government. The accumulation of wealth for an individual's personal benefit was forbidden.

After Mao's death in 1976, China began to embrace an economic system closer to our own. Today, therefore, private businesses now exist in the country and some businesspeople have built immense personal fortunes. Farming in the eastern part of the country has expanded greatly on the fertile plains, irrigated by China's great rivers as they push toward the China Sea. As you travel westward, away from the sea, though, the landscape becomes increasingly rugged and desertlike. Amazing differences distinguish the cities from the countryside: Chinese farmers use traditional methods not dependent on tractors and machines, while Chinese industry is more modern. Many of the farmers, who earn much smaller incomes than the city-dwellers, hope that their children will go to live and work in the cities.

Today, the entire world is watching to see what China's future will be. Some people believe that, with its enormous population, China will soon dominate the whole world. But others feel that the huge population numbers are a handicap and that the country remains too poor to grow and develop in any real way.

Zhang Meihua, Shi Shuilin, and Sem Dui Invite Us to China

Let's meet these kids so that we can share a little of their lives and learn about the different regions of China.

Zhang Meihua is a ten-year-old girl. Along with nine out of ten Chinese, she belongs to the Han ethnic group. Meihua lives in the northeast, very near the capital, Beijing. She absolutely adores her country and will tell us about its history.

Shi Shuilin and his friend Ma Liya live in Linxia, in the country's central region. Their lives are very different from those of the residents of Beijing. Shuilin is Han Chinese, while Liya is a Hui, one of the minority ethnic groups.

Zhang Meihua, Shi Shuilin, and Ma Liya all speak *putong hua*—the "common language" that we in the United States call Mandarin. It's used by 70 percent of the Chinese people. Meihua and Shuilin's families practice the traditional Chinese religion, whereas Liya is a Muslim.

Next, we'll board the bus in Lhasa and climb into the Himalaya mountains to the village of Sem Dui, a young Tibetan boy. Sem Dui speaks Tibetan, a language that is totally different from Mandarin. His life, too, is very different from those of the other Chinese kids we'll visit. And his religion is Buddhism, which he shares with most Tibetans.

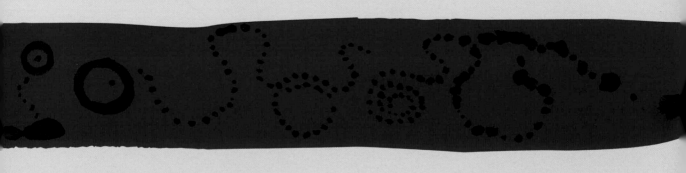

Zhang Meihua Goes to Beijing

Zhang Meihua is a ten-year-old girl. In Chinese, you put the family name, Zhang, in front of the first name. Her given name, Meihua, means "Flower of the Plum Tree" and is pronounced "May-hwa."

Meihua lives in a small apartment in one of the huge apartment buildings in Nanyuan, located a few miles from the capital, Beijing. Her parents were born in the coastal province of Zhejiang in the southeast of China. They came to the capital in the 1980s, drawn by the government, which gave them a place to live and, most important, jobs in its textile factories. China is the world's leading exporter of textiles (products made of woven cloth). It has no trouble selling these and other products throughout the world. Chinese workers earn less, in relative terms, than Americans. As a result, the cost of manufacturing these products is lower. In the United States, for example, Chinese goods cost less than American ones, even though they have to be sent by boat to our shores. This makes Chinese industry highly competitive, and it's continuing to grow and expand.

Meihua's paternal grandparents don't have a lot of money, so they share the family apartment. They weren't able to save anything or pay money into a retirement plan because when they were young, such a system did not yet exist. Now, however, some businesses provide for the retirement of their employees, and the state is setting up a new, modernized social welfare scheme that will pay higher benefits to workers.

The Chinese capital is Beijing. We Americans once called it Peking, which is a version of the same name. It unites two words that mean "Capital of the North." Long ago, there was also a "Capital of the South," Nanjing.

At its founding, Beijing was the capital of the Mongols, before becoming the Chinese capital in 1421. At that time, it was the home of the Ming Dynasty (a succession of supreme rulers belonging to the same family)—the emperors who reigned from 1368 to 1644. It ultimately became one of the capitals of the last Chinese dynasty, the Qing.

Today, Meihua and her class will visit the historic central city of Beijing. Everyone meets up early in the morning, decked out in the standard school uniform: orange T-shirt and white cap. The bus reaches the Beijing

suburbs. With blasts of its horn, it winds in, around, and through the strangling traffic jams and among the massive beehive of new buildings in progress. Meihua sits close to the bus driver. He explains to her that the road pattern is redrawn every six months, which makes it hard to move around Beijing. The lanes and passageways cut over the centuries are being destroyed, giving way to wider, more modern thoroughfares. The campaign to renovate and build never ceases. The city is constantly changing. The driver complains, "I've been driving in this city for fifteen years, but I can't recognize anything anymore!"

The Forbidden City

Finally the bus leaves the small group of children close to the Forbidden City.

In the past, when the Chinese emperor lived in the Forbidden City, only noblemen, advisers, and the Imperial family servants were allowed to enter this sanctum. The emperor's residence was the Gugong, or "Palace of the Emperors," the symbol of ancient China. Built between 1404 and 1420, the city is immense, with 9,999 buildings spread out over about 250 acres. Really, it's a city within a city! It's protected by 170-foot-wide moats and a 33-foot-high red wall. Red has deep significance in China. It represents happiness and, accordingly, can be found on many buildings.

A watchtower anchors the city at each corner of the ramparts. The four wooden buildings sit hunched on stone foundations. The name given to each pavilion represents one aspect of a happy destiny: the Pavilions of Harmony, Tranquility, Purity, and Longevity. These were the values most highly prized during the Imperial Era. The columns and walls are red, and tiles glazed in yellow—the color of the emperor—cover the roofs that craftsmen have sculpted into curves resembling pheasant wings. In Imperial times, no other structure in the city was allowed to equal

them in height or splendor. In fact, the emperor, called the "Son of Heaven," outshone everyone else in importance, and no one was allowed to even look him directly in the eye.

 ## The Temple of Heaven

Meihua's class now leaves the Forbidden City to visit the Temple of Heaven.

In China, as in some other civilizations, the natural elements—sky, earth, and water—are thought to be gods. They bestow life on humans or deal out death; from these divinities spring our blessings and calamities. Age-old Chinese rites instructed the emperors to honor them and to deal mercifully with the people. Accordingly, the emperors used to go twice a year to the Temple of Heaven, on the occasion of the summer and winter solstices, to give thanks to heaven and pray for abundant harvests.

Meihua and her classmates enter through the southern gate, which symbolizes earth. They proceed down a long passage that rises gradually as it leads toward the north, the symbol of heaven, and the main building, the Qiniandian, or "the Hall of Prayer for Abundant Harvests." This round pavilion standing at the center of a square esplanade is crowned with three roofs set one on top of the other and covered with blue glazed tiles. To enter, you have to climb three sets of stairs. This geometry embodies the Chinese conception of the universe as it was handed down in antiquity: a square earth set in a circular heaven.

Standing in the gardens of the temple's enormous park, which is five times larger than the Forbidden City, Meihua sees groups of men and women of all ages. These people consider the site a meeting place and a sanctuary. Older Chinese people, sometimes with their grandchildren in tow, join exercise groups that gather in the park, occasionally making use of scarves or sabers in their routines. Younger Chinese people arrive in couples, and some even bring boomboxes. They make the entire park resonate with traditional music. Others huddle around the players of mah-jongg, a game using Chinese dominoes on which flowers, swords, or Chinese characters are embossed. Still others sing passages taken from the Beijing Opera to accompaniments played on traditional instruments, such as percussion or the *erh-hu*, a kind of two-stringed violin.

Calligraphy, a Chinese Art

As they leave the precinct of the Temple of Heaven through the east gate, Meihua's group suddenly halts. There before them, an old man is bent over a foam brush. He dips it in a bucket of water and traces brief excerpts of ancient poems out on the ground.

Calligraphy is the art of beautiful writing. In China, the great calligraphers are as famous as the great painters.

The weather is still warm and the water quickly evaporates, so the first characters vanish even before the last ones are drawn. Yet the schoolchildren have time to recognize one of the poems they've learned by heart at school. It's "Eventide" by Li Bai, a celebrated poet who lived during the T'ang Dynasty, which ruled China for three hundred years between the seventh and the tenth centuries. Meihua recites out loud:

> *The moon rests at the foot of my bed*
> *And draws on the ground pools of frost.*
> *If I open my eyes, I see its brightness;*
> *If I close them, I think of my country.*

The calligrapher strives to draw his characters with great elegance. The beauty of Chinese characters lies in the positioning of the strokes; the most complex may need more than twenty of them. Just to read a newspaper, you'd have to memorize at least 3,000 characters. Unlike our alphabet, Chinese writing does not reproduce the sounds you make when you talk. Rather, it's an arrangement of strokes that directly signify an object or an idea.

After a quick but cheerful picnic near the Temple of Heaven, the bus takes the children to Tiananmen Square, whose name means "the Gate of Heavenly Peace."

Tiananmen is an enormous expanse which can hold two million people. The square is bursting with visitors—Chinese people, foreign tourists, and many groups of children from other schools thread their away around the street merchants, who call out to them to buy parasols and multicolored kites. Meihua must be careful to keep up with the school flag that's proudly flourished by Hong Ming, a schoolmate who received that honor because he scored 87 out of 100 on his quarterly exam. Meihua came in second, and she's disappointed at having come so close to receiving the perks that go to the top student.

Meihua sticks close to Hong Ming so the crowd won't carry her away. They head for the monument standing over the burial site of Mao Zedong. The line there is very long. Large numbers of Chinese come to pay their respects to the man they salute as the leader who made China a formidable power throughout the world.

M r. Xu, the history teacher who's chaperoning the class, has spoken many times about Mao.

Before the glass coffin in which Mao's mummified body is displayed, the teacher reminds them that it was here, in this square, that Mao proclaimed the creation of the People's Republic of China on October 1, 1949. The establishment of communist rule put an end to forty years of civil war and of struggle against the Japanese, who had occupied the country.

Meihua is well acquainted with the history of her nation, since Mr. Xu talks frequently at school about the sufferings that China experienced before 1949. At the start of the twentieth century, China struggled under the influence of the Western powers and Japan. In 1911, a revolution spurred the fall of the last emperor, Puyi, at the hands of the republican factions. However, much of China remained in poverty. The succeeding heads of government proved unable to relieve the destitution of the people. In 1921, the Communist Party was founded. Its goal was to give power to the working class and to pursue policies that promoted the people's well-being. At the time, there were very few Chinese communists. In 1927, they attempted uprisings in the cities, but they were harshly put down by the opposing Nationalist Party.

Mao reorganized the Communist Party to no longer rely on the workers in the cities, but rather on the farmers who made up the vast majority of the population. He established a true army, which gradually took up positions in the countryside. Then, in 1937, a major upheaval occurred: Japan invaded China. The Communists and Nationalists stopped fighting each other and joined to form a united front to resist the Japanese invasion. When the Second World War ended in 1945, Japan surrendered, leaving the two parties facing each other as adversaries. Civil war resumed. The Nationalists were vanquished in 1949 and chased from continental China to the island of Taiwan, where they founded the Republic of China. To this day, the leaders of the People's Republic of China (that is, communist China) consider Taiwan to be a province like any other in the nation, and they believe that, one day soon, the island will again become part of China.

 ## The Cultural Revolution

China has changed in many important ways since 1911. In a single century, it has become the sixth largest economic power in the world.

Meihua's grandparents have spoken to her about the problems the country had to overcome to achieve such a success, and of the errors that Mao made during the Cultural Revolution that lasted from 1966 to 1976. During this period, Mao dictated that every Chinese citizen had to become a revolutionary. He wanted every person to abandon the ancient values, such as family, religion, and tradition. This is what he meant when he advocated "putting politics at the helm of the state." The people were supposed to banish the bad leaders—officials who called themselves Communists, but who, Mao said, were really enemies of the communist movement. Mao's supporters asserted that he alone was capable of guiding the revolution.

To denounce the bad leaders, they launched a new revolution called the Cultural Revolution. The goal was to change the culture of the Chinese people and to transform their attitudes. Mao appealed to the

young to turn society upside down. As a result, millions of them joined the Red Guard. They roamed the country, destroying all vestiges of the past while claiming that their actions would ensure the birth of a new breed of human being. Great numbers of Chinese, especially intellectuals, suffered denunciation by their former colleagues, who accused them of wanting to return to old ways. They were punished and sent to reeducation camps, where they performed hard labor under very harsh conditions. Some were even sentenced to death. These years of civil war brought China to the brink of ruin, and daily life became extremely hard for everyone.

After Mao's death in 1976, his successors focused their energies on the growth of the Chinese economy. Mao's ideas were increasingly left by the wayside. Many of the leaders who had been imprisoned during the Cultural Revolution returned to power. Today, China is gradually distancing itself from communist ideals. Private firms are emerging, and Chinese individuals can become wealthy.

毛主席语录

The Little Red Book

The Worship of Ancestors and Gods

Once back at home, Meihua burns sticks of incense, in gratitude for her day. She places an apple before the altar of her ancestors—a small table holding wooden tablets bearing the ancestors' names, a bowl used for burning the incense sticks, and food offerings.

In China, people believe that ancestors and gods watch over the people living here on earth. By giving offerings and honoring them, the people gain their protection. That's why an altar of the ancestors is placed in each home. It reminds each individual of her origins and of the importance of family. Ancestor worship dates back to Confucius, a sage who lived in the sixth century BCE. Confucianism is not really a religion as we understand the term, since it does not worship any god. Rather, it's a moral doctrine and a set of rules that govern the relationships between the emperor and his subjects, and those between family members, ancestors who have passed on after death, relatives, and children. Subjects owe obedience to the emperor, just as sons must obey their fathers.

In the beginning, the emperor alone practiced ancestor worship. The ritual then spread throughout the entire society. But during the period of communist rule, Mao's partisans fought against the Confucian doctrine and other religions which were deemed to be "poison." Yet the Chinese have always adhered to this practice, which has sometimes mixed with Taoism.

Taoism was created by Lao Tzu, a sage who also lived during the sixth century BCE, at about the same time as Confucius. According to Lao Tzu, man must find his *tao* (a Chinese word meaning "road or path"), his place in the universe. Above all, man must refrain from acting so as to disrupt the harmony of the world or to cause harm to life as it's lived in nature. For example, each person must refuse to go along with social or

political rules if they're unjust. Followers must reject corruption and flattery and refuse to carry out the orders of a leader if they believe that they are harmful. Harmony alone is the goal. Harmony is composed of a female element, the yin, and a male one, the yang, each of which forms the perfect complement of the other.

As time passed, Taoism became a true religion. The Taoists venerated various gods, for example the earth god, who gives food; the god of water, who causes the crops to grow; and the god of heaven, who, like the ancestors, vigilantly attends to the happiness of families. Through meditation, the contemplation of nature, and the observance of very precise daily rituals, believers protect themselves from harmful acts and disease. Such practices promise to guide you to immortality. In fact, Taoist tradition says that the spirits of the vanished family members lie, not figuratively but literally, in wooden tablets, such as those honoring the names of Meihua's ancestors.

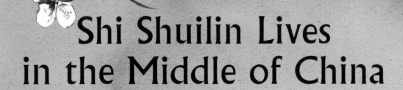

Shi Shuilin Lives in the Middle of China

Shi Shuilin is a young boy of twelve. With his older sister, he's in the process of doing a puzzle that his mother brought back from the market in Linxia, the city where he lives in the Gansu Province in the middle of China. This puzzle is a plastic map of China, and with it Shuilin can review his geography lessons in a fun way. He has to put the 23 provinces of China (including Taiwan) and the five autonomous regions in their proper places.

The term "autonomous regions" refers to areas populated by minority ethnic groups, such as the Xinjiang Autonomous Region, where the Uighurs, a Muslim people, are especially numerous. In the autonomous regions, the inhabitants are the ones who are supposed to make most of the governing decisions. In reality, though, the most important of these decisions are made in Beijing.

Shi Shuilin and His Sister, Bao

Shuilin is particularly lucky to be able to play with his older sister, Bao. Why is this? It's very rare for a Chinese child to have a brother or a sister! Starting in the 1970s, Chinese leaders decided that a strong surge in the population could pull down the economic growth of the country. Should the population become too large, the risk was that the people would no longer be able to find jobs or housing or be able to get high-quality health care. So the government arrived at a decision: In the major cities, couples could now have only one child. In Linxia, however, far

from Beijing, this policy is observed less strictly. So the parents of Bao and Shuilin were able to have two kids.

The "single child" policy was met with a great deal of opposition and hostility, especially in the rural areas. Among the farmers, tradition held that a son, and not a daughter, should inherit the entire wealth of the parents upon their deaths. And in the poorer regions, sons are supposed to provide for their parents' retirement. So when the first child born to a family was a girl, the parents absolutely insisted on having a second! Beginning in 1979, and up through the 1980s and 1990s, the birth of a second child meant violating the law—and, in fact, a number of couples with three or four children were prosecuted and some families were broken up. But the introduction of ultrasound scanning, which can determine a baby's gender well before birth, made it possible for couples to decide to pursue the pregnancy only if the baby was male. If not, they sometimes chose to have an abortion.

These convolutions and complications led to a breach of the natural balance in births. At present, there are not enough girls in China. At the start of the twenty-first century, 111 boys were born for every 100 girls—a trend that is becoming more pronounced. To remedy this growing imbalance, some provinces now prohibit tests of the gender of the fetus before birth, in order to prevent mothers from aborting them.

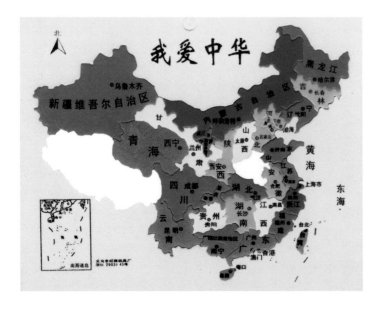

A puzzle showing China
and its provinces and regions

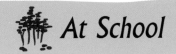

Shuilin is in the sixth grade, the final year before junior high school.

In his Chinese-language class, he has already learned to write his characters, carefully following the order in which the strokes must be made. To increase his vocabulary, he constantly memorizes and writes new characters. He has also learned a number of classic poems, which his teacher has the students recite as they stand before the class. In addition, the schoolchildren study mathematics, science, and history, and play sports. They also sing patriotic songs. Finally, they take courses in political ethics, where they must recite by heart precepts and slogans of the Communist Party.

Shuilin does not want to disappoint his parents, who hope that a strong education will make his life better than theirs. His father works at the Telecommunications Administration, and his mother is a nurse's aid at a hospital. In addition to his daytime classes, his parents pay for organized evening study, during which a teacher gives his best pupils extra practice. The success of the students is important for the teacher, too, since his salary depends on their achievements. If his students get good grades, he gets paid more. Shuilin's parents have even told their son that if his quarterly test scores fall below a satisfactory standard, he'll have to study on Saturdays, too! For this reason, some of his schoolmates even take classes during vacations, so that they always make progress. He has to work hard, since he enters secondary school next year. Only the best students gain admission to the most renowned schools.

Even though Shuilin sometimes dislikes his parents' rules, he knows that he's lucky. Once, in front of a restaurant, he saw two dirty, badly dressed children begging for a few coins. His father told him that the parents of such kids are often poor farmers who have come to work in the cities. In fact, many families drawn by economic growth migrate to the cities in the hope of getting work. One must obtain a certificate of employment and a temporary residence permit, yet many fail to get them, even though that documentation is a prerequisite for enrolling children in public schools. People who don't find work do not receive any government assistance. They live an uncertain, hand-to-mouth existence, sometimes even in the street, and their children don't get to go to school.

Should Shuilin Head East?

Shuilin does not yet know what profession he wants to practice when he grows up, but he wouldn't mind being an engineer for the Telecommunications Administration, like his father.

To have such a job, he must improve his grades in school. He knows the competition is stiff. The teacher says so every day and, when he returns home each evening, his parents are there to monitor his studies. Each time he receives a poor grade, his father reminds him that he is not the only one who wants to head east to Shanghai or Canton, where the standard of living is higher.

Many young Chinese living in central or western China hope to emigrate from their region. On television and in magazines, they see images of the modern cities of the east, with their skyscrapers,

highways, and swarms of cars, while the rest of the country moves around by bicycles, buses, and trucks. In the "special economic zones" (immense industrial parks built in the east), gigantic factories make products intended for sale in foreign countries: ships, machine tools, clothing, shoes, toys—the list is endless. While salaries are higher in the east than in the rest of the country, they're still very low compared with Western nations—which means that Chinese goods can easily be sold to the Europeans or Americans, for whom they are not very expensive. As a result, Chinese trade has been increasing at a spectacular rate.

These drastic economic changes are relatively new, given that the Chinese had to wait until Deng Xiaoping returned to power in 1977 before the Chinese economy could be modernized. Deng had been a highly influential leader in the Communist Party, but he was unseated and swept aside during the Cultural Revolution. Starting in 1977, and until his death in 1997, Deng devised an economic program very different from the one advocated by Mao's circle. Prior to that period, only the Chinese state could carry out foreign trade. Deng's reforms, however, made private businesses possible.

S huilin has learned that the largest group in China is the one to which he belongs, the Han.

There are more than 1.2 billion ethnic Han, the largest ethnic group in China (and in the world!). The first traces of the group's history were found in the basins of the Huang and Yangtze (or Chang Jiang) Rivers (the Yellow and Blue Rivers, respectively). It was there that the first farmers settled nearly 10,000 years ago. Also in these regions, the first rulers came to power 6,000 years ago, and then the first dynasties ruled more than 4,000 years ago.

Not all Chinese people are ethnic Han, though. Shuilin has a very good friend at school named Ma Liya. She covers her hair with a small white veil, which indicates that she is Muslim. She belongs to another ethnic group, the Hui. Shuilin is only a moderately good student, but Ma Liya is brilliant. The teacher has placed her in the front row, with the best students.

Shi Shuilin comes home each evening, since he lives near the school. Ma Liya, though, is a boarding student. Her parents live 12 miles away, and the school buses do not go to her village. She's often sad when she thinks about her family. It's at those times that Shuilin stays to talk with her. Ma Liya tells him about the

Hui community, which makes up half of the 1.5 million inhabitants of the city.

The Hui religion is Islam. The first Muslims entered China in the seventh century over the so-called silk roads. Most Muslims were merchants who traveled across Central Asia to trade the products made in the Arabic Middle East for Asian goods, such as silk, which were highly prized. During the thirteenth century, a large population of Arabian and Persian merchants came to settle in the Chinese northwest. They made Linxia the Muslim hub of this region. Today, the minarets of many mosques look over the rooftops of the city. Every day, you can hear the Muslim calls to prayer.

Of the 56 ethnic groups that make up the nation of China, 10 are Muslim, like the Hui. Young Hui children also learn Arabic in secondary school, which allows them to deepen their understanding of their holy text, the Koran. Some people use it to carry on trade with Arabic countries. Despite this, however, the first language of the Hui remains Chinese.

The Spring Festival

The children are excited that the Spring Festival is approaching. That means it's time to gather the family together, to have fun, and to feast.

This festival falls on the first day of the lunar calendar, which differs from the solar-based Western calendar. The lunar calendar is based on the time between two new moons, called a "lunar month." In Chinese astrology, each year bears the name of an animal: rat, ox, tiger, hare, dragon, snake, horse, goat, monkey, rooster, dog, or pig. The Chinese attribute specific powers to each of these animals, and these powers are believed to affect the destiny of the people born under the various signs.

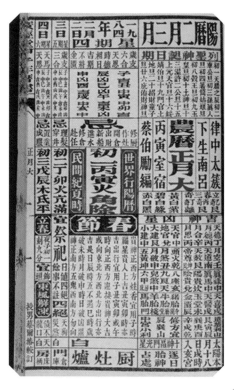

In 1911, the republican authorities adopted the solar calendar for the government, in order to place them on the same footing as the international community and ease relations with other nations. Nevertheless, the lunar calendar is still used for traditional holidays. The Spring Festival, which marks the first full moon of the lunar year, is actually the Chinese New Year. It falls between the end of January and the beginning of February of our calendar.

To prepare for the festival, Shuilin's mother starts by cleaning the house completely, since no housework will be done for the next three days. No one would thing of sweeping away the good fortune that will enter the home on New Year's Day!

The last day of the year has finally arrived. Shuilin watches as his father burns the image of the god of the hearth, who ascends to the sky to make his report on the family's good or bad deeds to Yu-huang, the Jade Emperor, the Governor of Heaven. To prevent him from issuing a bad report, the family bakes sugar donuts covered with a sticky syrup that will lock his lips together!

In Chinese, the word for "fish" is *yu*, and the same sound also means "abundance." Shuilin's mother prepares a fish, which symbolizes the abundance that will bless their home at the New Year. The entire family makes *jiaozi* (dumplings) shaped like half-moons. It's a festive dish. Since *jiao* means "get together," many people have to join together to make it.

The dough is made of flour and water, and the filling is ground pork (or mutton) and vegetables flavored with garlic, sesame oil, and the "five spices." In truth, this traditional blend is made up of seven spices—ginger, pepper, cinnamon, star anise, clove, cardamom, and licorice. The dough is divided into several balls, each of which is rolled into a rope shape that is cut into small pieces. Next, the pieces are squashed with the palm of the hand, then rolled out using a small rolling pin to make them round. The filling is placed in the center, and the little turnover is folded closed. The edges are fastened with the fingers, so as to give the dumpling the shape of a *yuan bao* (a silver ingot weighing three pounds and shaped like a half-moon). The *jiaozi* are then cooked in boiling water and served with a sauce made of vinegar, soy sauce, crushed garlic, and sesame oil. The *jiaozi* are made the day before the New Year begins and must be completed before midnight. They are then enjoyed at the moment when the old year changes to the new. When eaten, this small "ingot" enables each person to "welcome fortune and become wealthy," as the Chinese say.

After the meal, Shuilin and his sister impatiently wait for the giving of the *hong bao*, red envelopes containing New Year's money. After that, the family will set off firecrackers in front of the house. The noise from the small explosions is supposed to frighten evil spirits and make them run away, so that they will not enter the home. In large urban centers, though, this practice is now forbidden, in order to prevent fires.

A Recipe for Jiaozi

For 35 to 40 dumplings:

Dough:
    2 cups flour
    1 cup water

Filling:
    1 $\frac{1}{4}$ cups ground pork or mutton
    $\frac{1}{2}$ cup Chinese cabbage, thinly sliced and soaked in salt
    1 pinch of the "five spices"
    2 bunches fresh coriander, finely chopped
    2 teaspoons fresh ginger, peeled and minced
    2 cloves garlic, finely chopped
    1 tablespoon soy sauce
    1 tablespoon sesame oil
    1 egg

Mix the flour and water together until the dough becomes elastic. Let it rest for one hour. In the meantime, mix together all of the filling ingredients. Roll the dough into a rope shape and cut into pieces. Flatten the pieces out with the palm of your hand, and then spread them out using a rolling pin. Place filling on the dough rounds and close the turnover. Place the turnovers in small batches in a large saucepan filled with boiling water and cook until they become translucent. Drain, then keep warm in a cloth towel.

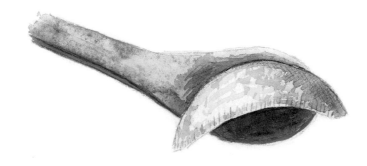

A Puppet Show

The next day, since school is out for a week, Shuilin goes for a walk in the streets of the city. He meets up with his neighborhood buddies, who are playing nearby. Suddenly, they hear blasts of gongs and cymbals coming from a small alley.

In front of the red columns of a Taoist temple, a kind of small wooden castle has been set up. The elderly bring folding chairs, and younger people sit on the ground. The elders know the most famous scenes by heart, because puppet shows are frequently given in China. Everyone knows the stories they tell. Whole families flock to the shows, but they don't always listen to every word. Instead they talk while waiting for the passages they love the best. Some of the performances can last for three hours!

This show is being presented in homage to Yu-huang, the Jade Emperor and principal divinity of the Taoists. The characters are marionettes 12 inches high. A puppeteer controls each one: he moves the arms and legs with one hand, and he uses the other to animate the head. Some puppets have jointed mouths and eyebrows. The puppets can hold weapons, fans, or parasols. They wear richly embroidered costumes, and their faces are painted in various colors that represent their characters. To the right of the small wooden castle, the orchestra carefully follows the movements of these actors of wood and cloth.

Around the drummer, who conducts the orchestra, Shuilin finds the percussionists, the violinists, and the oboe players. When he first spies two of the characters, a monkey sporting a white-and-gold face and a figure wearing a pig mask, Shuilin immediately recognizes the tale. It's an ancient story. The Westward Voyage recounts the adventures of a monk who travels to India to bring back some sacred texts. His bodyguards are Sun Wukong, the Monkey King, and the Pig of the Eight Vows. This episode tells of the moment when the Spirit of the White Skeleton turns into a girl in order to divert the pig. However, he's unmasked by Sun Wukong, who chases him away. The marionettes are very lifelike! They walk, run, and pirouette in the air, before the puppet masters catch them in mid-flight. The Spirit of the White Skeleton even contains a mechanical device that makes it possible to change his face. Shuilin marvels at the show. When they're manipulated with skill, the marionettes are as wonderfully expressive as flesh-and-blood actors.

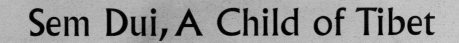

Sem Dui, A Child of Tibet

Summer vacation is approaching. Like many other young Tibetans, Sem Dui is going to leave the regional capital, Lhasa, where he's at boarding school. He'll go by bus to his small village, Mendui, and his family's home. He's proud of his country, culture, language, and customs, which are very different from those of Meihua and Shuilin.

Tibet is located in the Himalaya mountains, the highest mountain chain in the world. Entry into the territory is difficult. As a result, it has long remained independent. Indeed, under the last dynasty of Chinese emperors, the Qing, Tibet existed in virtually total isolation, partly because the emperors no longer possessed the military capabilities they needed to make the Tibetans respect their authority. During the twentieth century, however, the region underwent cataclysmic changes. To the south of the Himalayas, India gained its independence, and, to the north, the Chinese Communists seized power in 1949. At that point, for economic and military reasons, Tibet became the focus of both countries, for the Himalayas formed a kind of natural barrier between them. In 1950, the Chinese Communists launched efforts to conquer Tibet. In their mind, Tibet actually belonged to China. The tragedy of this campaign reached huge proportions: More than one million Tibetans who attempted to resist Chinese forces were killed.

Since that time, Tibet has been transformed into one of the autonomous regions of the People's Republic of China. Its official name is the Autonomous Region of Xizang.

Xizang is populated by a minority ethnic group, the Tibetans. They speak a language different from that spoken by the Han—Tibetan—which has nothing in common with Chinese. Like most Tibetans, Sem Dui practices Buddhism.

Buddhism was begun more than 2,500 years ago by Siddartha Gautama, a prince of the Sakya family. Once his eyes opened to the poverty and misery of the world, he abandoned his palace, his princely title, and all his belongings. By remaining in poverty, and through meditation, he became the Buddha (or the "Awakened One") Sakyamuni.

The Buddha teaches a way of life that is nonviolent and respectful of all beings. His doctrine is founded on the belief that all living beings are caught up in an endless cycle of rebirths in various forms, whether human or animal. The essential nature of each new life reflects the good or evil acts that the individual performed in his or her previous one. Yet life is the province of sorrow; it is hard to bear all of the misfortune that one sees everywhere, the Buddha said. To escape the suffering that these rebirths cause, Buddhism points to a path that leads to spiritual awakening—a state of complete wisdom, or "nirvana." Long after the life of the Buddha, during the eighteenth century, the Indian master Padmasambhava brought Buddhism to Tibet.

Knowledge of the sacred texts is taught by the lamas, not all of whom are monks. They may marry and have children, while monks must observe the rules of the monasteries.

 ## Sem Dui Visits the Potala Palace in Lhasa

Sem Dui's secondary school is located in the very center of Lhasa. The ice-cream seller next door is invaded every afternoon by hordes of schoolchildren in uniform. Sem Dui is dressed in the traditional red and white.

Lhasa is about 11,500 feet above sea level, right in the heart of the Himalayas. The city has long remained mysterious, since very few foreigners were fortunate enough to visit it. The kings and Dalai Lamas (the religious and political leaders of the Tibetan Buddhists) wanted the country free of outside influence. To this end, they refused entry to almost all foreigners. Since 1981, though, all that has changed, and the city now welcomes tourists. Sem Dui sees them strolling around the most impressive monument in the city, the Potala. Their eyes are open wide, and their cameras hang ready on shoulder straps.

Like most Tibetans, Sem Dui has already visited the Potala, which is both a palace and a monastery. It's built on Red Mountain and dominates the city.

From the outside, you see an immense assemblage of white and red structures arranged over a height of 13 floors. The whole edifice measures 1,200 feet in length by 384 feet in height. The floors of the "Red Palace" are reserved for the monks, while those of the "White Palace" are occupied by the government. Once inside, you wander through a labyrinth of narrow corridors to reach the monks' chambers, which are lit from yak butter burning in small lamps. These sacred rooms house treasures: the golden chortens. These are monuments that hold sacred relics—parts of the bodies of the Dalai Lamas from the past. The sancta are decorated with very ancient paintings of gods, goddesses, and the monsters that guard the heavens with their terrifying gazes. Sem Dui is not afraid. He has been familiar with these beings since childhood and knows they are there to keep out harmful spirits. During long night vigils, his family tells tales and legends of these beings.

In one imposing room stands the throne of the Dalai Lama, whose name, taken from the Mongolian language, means "ocean of wisdom." The current Dalai Lama, Tenzin Gyatso, refused to recognize China's violent imposition of power after 1950. He fled to India, where he has remained in exile since 1959. This means, of course, that he no longer lives in the Potala.

The Potala is now a museum and is classified among humanity's official treasures. Sacred Buddhist texts are kept there, covered with large wrappings of yellow silk and zealously guarded for their inestimable worth. Poor visitors bring offerings of yak butter, with which they fill the many lamps that illuminate the statues of the divinities. The more wealthy visitors offer money. Sem Dui gives his yak butter offering and recites prayers. The atmosphere of the Potala inspires, and is inspired by, contemplation. Pilgrims come in search of benediction and worthiness, both for this life and those to follow, since Tibetan Buddhists believe in reincarnation—the idea that, after death, they will live another life in another body.

The Road to Mendui

The land that nourishes Tibetan culture has a surface area of 2,356,000 square miles, or eight times the area of Texas. It is significantly larger than the Tibetan Autonomous Region by itself, which encompasses only 744,000 square miles, or, in this case, a little less than three times the area of Texas.

Tibetan villages are unique and easily identified. Above the entranceway, a small oven in the shape of a chorten (a Buddhist monument symbolizing earth, fire, and water) releases smoke from burning juniper wood. The *lungta*, or "wind horse," flags printed with the prayers that the winds carry to the divinities, are anchored to the roof.

To return home to his village, Sem Dui takes a small bus. It's packed with travelers. The passengers rush to store their luggage and packages, which contain everything the villagers have bought in town: fabrics, saucepans, duvets, horse harnesses, and much more. "*Tashi delek!* Hello!" they cry. People greet each other, share the latest news, and take out their thermoses of tea flavored with yak butter, all while waiting patiently for the bus to start up. They also spin their small prayer wheels—metal cylinders with handles that hold a mantra (a prayer) wound around the prayer-wheel shaft. When a Buddhist spins the wheel, he arouses the energy of the mantra, so that it flies unfurled to the world of the spirits. It is a form of prayer.

Two monks ride on the bus. They recite their mantras using their beads, called *mala*. Having made their pilgrimage to the Potala, they're leaving Lhasa to embark on a series of small journeys that will ultimately lead back to the monastery.

The bus skims along prairies covered with wheat and barley. This year, the weather has been mild, and the crops are ripe and ready for the scythe. In some fields, villagers cut the stalks with billhooks. Children mold the bales and load them onto the backs of small donkeys. The people spread the harvest over the road that crosses the village so that it will dry, and so that the trucks rolling over the road will crush their crops and separate the individual grains. The road starts to climb. It's quite narrow, and, in some places, two vehicles cannot pass each other. When that happens, one of them has to pull back. To reach Mendui, the bus has to go through a pass three miles high— and it's not even the highest one! The landscape changes; the grass is indeed green, but at this altitude, farming is no longer possible. You can see herds of yaks, sheep, and goats grazing.

"Soso lha gyalo! Soso lha gyalo!" **("The gods are victorious!"),** the bus driver cries out as the bus crosses the pass. Small bits of paper resembling confetti fly out of the bus windows. They're covered with drawings of horses and prayers: "Thanks to the gods for letting us traverse

their realm without incident!" The road descends once again. Sem Dui feels happy. He is accustomed to the altitude, yet sometimes still gets headaches from it.

One last crossing through a mountain stream (since bridges don't exist everywhere), and there it is—his village, which stands silhouetted against the horizon. The two-story houses set against the mountain stand out in profile. Little white curtains flap against the wooden window frames. The eight signs that traditionally bring luck and happiness to the family are painted on them: the goldfish, the endless knot, the parasol, the wheel of life, the shell, the victory banner, the lotus, and the bowl of treasures. Multi-colored prayer flags flutter over the flat roofs, on which wood and bricks fashioned from yak dung are stored for heating. And each house's domain includes the yard where the animals are kept.

🌱 A Farming Culture

Sem Dui's mother and father wait impatiently for his arrival. They make many financial sacrifices so that he can go school.

School is expensive. There are the clothes, the supplies, and the bus trips to pay for. Sem Dui can't afford the supplementary classes that would place him among the top students. He's also expected to perform his share of the work at home, since everyone works, including children. Farming and livestock breeding is an endless job! But when he returns, it's time to celebrate. His mother makes him *momo*, dumplings filled with yak meat. Then, tomorrow, he'll go say hello to the other members of the family.

Already, Sem Dui has a job. His brother, Norbu, asked him to help bring the yak herd back to the autumn pastures. He exchanges his school uniform for the traditional *chuba*, a large leather coat. A bag of *tsampa*, or grilled barley flour, a few bricks of dried tea leaves, a little dried yak meat, and . . . that's it! Our young Tibetan is ready for the trip! He'll get water on the way, since the Himalayas form a natural reservoir. From these mountains flow the biggest rivers in Asia: the Chinese Yangtze, the Indian Brahmaputra, and the Vietnamese Mekong.

Life is harsh for Tibetan shepherds. They must lead their flocks far from the village and frequently change pastures, always at very high altitudes. They are away from the village for months at a time. Even in summer, the nights are extremely cool. The wind blows, and their canvas tents are not very substantial. They make their fires in portable stoves using dried yak dung, an efficient fuel. There's not much variety to the food, though. From female yaks they get milk, butter, and meat. As for everything else, they have to barter with the farmers in the valley, who produce cereals for the *tsampa* and the *chang*, or beer, and a few vegetables. They buy rice and fruit in town.

Sem Dui loves his brother, and they talk for hours together. Norbu wants to know everything about the things Sem Dui has seen in the city. Both of them feel that the world is changing, even in Tibet.

In fact, Tibet is changing very rapidly. New roads are being built, and even a railroad line—the highest in the world. It will connect Lhasa to Xining, the capital of Qinghai. This worries the Tibetans, who are devoted to their culture, their language, and their country with all of its unique features. They are afraid of the gradual loss of their cultural identity. For that reason, Sem Dui has mixed feelings: From the bottom of his heart, he wants to preserve the traditions of his people, but at the same time, he would like to improve his own well-being.

Photographic Credits:

Library of Congress Cataloging-in-Publication Data has been applied for.
ISBN 10: 0-8109-5735-3
ISBN 13: 978-0-8109-5735-0

Printed and bound in France
by Pollina - n° L40237D
10 9 8 7 6 5 4 3 2 1

HNA ▪▪▪▪▪
harry n. abrams, inc.
a subsidiary of La Martinière Groupe
115 West 18th Street
New York, NY 10011
www.hnabooks.com